Ministering in the Gifts
of the Spirit

VOLUME 8

Ministering
in the
Gifts *of the*
Spirit

A spiritual gift is given to each of
us as a means of helping the entire
church. 1 Corinthians 12:7

....

A 30-day Devotional Bible Study
for Individuals or Groups.

....

Dr. Larry Keefauver

CREATION
H O U S E
Orlando, FL

MINISTERING IN THE GIFTS OF THE SPIRIT by Larry Keefauver

Published by Creation House
Strang Communications Company
600 Rinehart Road
Lake Mary, FL 32746

Web site: http://www.creationhouse.com

Unless otherwise noted, all Scripture quotations are the Holy Bible, New Living Translation, copyright © 1996. Used by permission of Tyndale House Publishers, Inc., Wheaton, IL 60189. All rights reserved.

8901234 8765432

Contents

Introduction

Welcome to this devotional study guide that will assist you in welcoming the Holy Spirit into your life. This is one of eight devotional studies related to the *Holy Spirit Encounter Bible.* Though not absolutely necessary, it is recommended that you obtain a copy of the *Holy Spirit Encounter Bible* for your personal use with this study guide. We make this recommendation because the same translation used in this guide, the *New Living Translation,* is also used in the *Holy Spirit Encounter Bible.*

It is also recommended that you choose the study guides in this series in the sequence that best meets your spiritual needs. So please don't feel that you must go through them in any particular order. Each study guide has been developed for individual, group, or class use.

Additional instruction has been included at the end of this guide for those desiring to use it in class or group settings.

Because the purpose of this guide is to help readers encounter the person of the Holy Spirit through the Scriptures, individuals going through it are invited to use it for personal daily devotional reading and study. Each daily devotional is structured to:

❖ Probe deeply into the Scriptures.

❖ Examine one's own personal relationship with the Holy Spirit.

❖ Discover biblical truths about the Holy Spirit.

❖ Encounter the person of the Holy Spirit continually in one's daily walk with God.

We pray that this study guide will be an effective tool for equipping you to study God's Word and to encounter the wonderful third person of the triune God—the Holy Spirit.

N *ow there are different kinds of spiritual gifts, but it is the same Holy Spirit who is the source of them all (1 Cor. 12:4).*

The Holy Spirit gives believers spiritual gifts for the purpose of ministering to Christ's body and the lost in the world. While His gifts may bless and encourage us because of being used powerfully in ministry, they should never give anyone reason to boast or take pride in the gift. Gifts are given to be given away, and God will give through the humble.

So, if we want to be used, we must draw a distinction between gifts, talents, and skills. To help do this, read through the list of qualities below. Choose which quality best describes a gift and list it in the gift column. Then list those that best describe talents or skills in their respective columns.

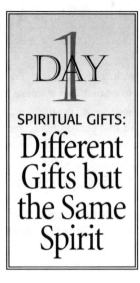

DAY 1

SPIRITUAL GIFTS:

Different Gifts but the Same Spirit

Spiritual Gifts		Talents or Skills
	A. earned	A
	B. learned	B
	C. deserved	C
D	D. grace	
E	E. undeserved	
F	F. free	
	G. proud	G
H	H. humble	
	I. exalts self	J
	J. edifies others	
3	K. exercised at will	K
L	L. exercised at His will	

Now look your list over. The qualities that best describe spiritual gifts are D, F, H, J, and L. Why? Because the Greek word for gifts, *charismata*, is rooted in the word for grace—which means, "that which is freely given."

Though we are often equipped to minister the gifts by others who can model their ways of operation, we can't earn, deserve, or learn the gifts. But even in our training, the right style, behaviors, words, and methods of others can never substitute for the free power of God.

So in this study we will discover what the charismatic gifts of the Holy Spirit are. And we will look at the Spirit's *way* in ministry. To minister means *to serve* not *to be served!* So let's begin.

The Spirit may choose to use our talents and skills empowered by His gifts to minister, but He doesn't need them. What He needs is our humble obedience.

> *The Holy Spirit seeks willing, surrendered, and available vessels to pour His gifts into for the work of His ministry.*

To summarize:

❖ The source of spiritual gifts is the Holy Spirit.
❖ Spiritual gifts are freely given, not earned.
❖ Gifts are for ministry, not personal glory.
❖ The gifts of the Spirit aren't personal possessions. They are powerful abilities entrusted to us for ministry.

Ask yourself . . .

❖ What gifts would you like the Holy Spirit to minister through you?
gift of teaching

❖ How can you avoid possessing or taking pride in the gifts?
by always look to the Holy Spirit in working Gods will in my life

Write a prayer thanking God for the gifts of the Holy Spirit:

Thank you Lord for your mercy and mercy you have given. I Pray that they ache clean. Humbly the gift being glory to God and your name. Amen

A *spiritual gift is given to each of us as a means of helping the entire church (1 Cor. 12:7).*

At times some believers feel the church doesn't need them. They feel inadequate, unequipped, and insignificant. Have you ever felt that way?

If you've ever felt "useless," or that the Holy Spirit would never use you, then you have believed a lie. Because not only *will* the Holy Spirit use you to minister to others, He has already imparted a ministry gift to you. Think about it! As a willing, obedient vessel, the

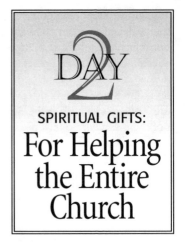

SPIRITUAL GIFTS:

For Helping the Entire Church

Holy Spirit wants to use you to minister in a number of different gifts. But every believer has at least one gift from the Holy Spirit that He uses often to minister through. *To each of us* means that God's Spirit imparts *to each of us* a spiritual gift for serving His body.

Check any of the following statements you may have ever made about ministering the gifts:

❑ God could never use me to minister in that gift.

❑ I'm not worthy to minister in that gift.

❑ Since I've failed in ministering in that gift in the past, the Spirit can't use me again.

❑ I'm inadequately equipped to minister in a spiritual gift.

❑ Ministering in the gifts is for pastors and leaders, not for me.

If you truly believe any of these statements, you are truly wrong! Why? The whole body is empowered by the Holy Spirit to minister in His gifts. In 1 Corinthians 14:26, Paul writes about orderly worship and ministry. In your own words, summarize what Paul is saying:

_____

_____

Reject any false beliefs you've held in the past, now! And embrace the move of the Holy Spirit in and through you.

The Holy Spirit will use you to minister to others as you are willing to fully surrender to His will. The gifts of the Holy Spirit are given to help others. And He wants to use you!

Below is a list of some of the gifts of the Spirit. Circle those that you desire from Him for ministry:

Wise advice	Special knowledge
Faith	Power to heal
Power to perform miracles	Ability to prophesy
Discernment	Unknown languages
Interpretation of unknown languages	

The Holy Spirit empowers His gifts in each church to minister to the needs of that body and the surrounding community. He can and will empower you to meet these needs.

Ask yourself . . .

❖ How is your spiritual gifting currently helping the church?

❖ What new ways do you desire the Spirit to minister through you?

Write a prayer asking God's Spirit to inspire you to desire all that He has for you in ministry:

_____

_____

_____

_____

_____

*I*t is the one and only Holy Spirit who distributes these gifts. He alone decides which gift each person should have (1 Cor. 12:11).

DAY 3

SPIRITUAL GIFTS:
The Spirit Alone Decides

We live in a time in which the world view is: "Just do it!" Or, "You can make it happen!" But we can't manipulate, control, or make spiritual gifts happen. Yes, we must be willing and available to the Holy Spirit to do what He wants. But the Holy Spirit is sovereign.

The Holy Spirit alone decides what gifts to give and how to use them in ministry. Here are some verses that reveal the sovereignty of God. Read each one and jot down what it means:

Romans 9:15–16_____

Micah 7:18 _____

Romans 9:18–19_____

Lamentations 3:37_____

Matthew 6:25–33_____

Job 38_____

It is the Holy Spirit who decides which gift you will be given to minister to the needs of others in and out of the church. So instead of asking Him for what *you* want, start seeking what *He* desires to do both in and through you.

Take some time to think of the needs in your home church. Then think of the needs of some non-Christians you know, and list them.

1._____

2._____

3._____

4._____

5._____

6._____

Now begin interceding for these needs. Ask the Holy Spirit to reveal which needs He desires to have met through you. Then pray for whatever gifts He wants to impart to you for that ministry and service.
How do we minister in the gifts of the Spirit? *With an attitude!* That's right,

ministering the gifts begins with the right attitude. So read each of the following passages and jot down the attitudes the Holy Spirit honors and endows with His gifts:

The Text	The Attitude
Philippians 2:5–11	_humble + obedience_
Psalm 51:7–13	
Psalm 37:3–9	
Micah 6:8	
James 4:7–10	
Romans 12:1–2	
Romans 13:8–10	
Matthew 22:37–40	
Luke 4:4, 8, 12	
Philippians 4:8–9	
Proverbs 4:23–27	

The recurring theme in these passages is *servanthood.* God uses servants to minister in the power of His Spirit (Acts 2:18).

> *The Holy Spirit sovereignly empowers His gifts through servants.*

Ask yourself . . .

❖ How is the Holy Spirit at work in your spirit to give you the heart of a servant?

❖ What godly attitudes need to grow in your life so the Spirit can use you more?

Write a prayer asking God's Spirit to create in you a servant's heart:

_____

_____

_____

God has given gifts to each of you from his great variety of spiritual gifts. Manage them well so that God's generosity can flow through you (1 Pet. 4:10).

Prodigality is a good redemptive word. The prodigality of God is revealed in every area of our spiritual lives. The word speaks of the abundance, prosperity, overflowing provision, limitless mercy, and infinite grace of God. His abundant grace is also manifested in the spiritual gifts that He releases to the church. They come to us in great measure and variety.

DAY 4

SPIRITUAL GIFTS:

Let God's Generosity Flow

What evidences of the prodigality of God have you witnessed? Each statement below speaks of it. Complete each sentence with a testimony of how you have seen God's abundance in that aspect of life.

❖ In creation, I see God's prodigality in _____

_____.

❖ In salvation, I see God's prodigality in _____

_____.

❖ In healing, I see God's prodigality in _____

_____.

❖ In my family, I see God's prodigality in _____

_____.

❖ In the church, I see God's prodigality in_____

_____.

❖ In ministry, I see God's prodigality in _____

_____.

❖ In meeting my needs, I see God's prodigality in _____

_____.

❖ In spiritual gifts, I see God's prodigality in_____

_____.

God's great prodigality of spiritual gifts is entrusted to us to serve another's needs. But we must manage them well so His generosity can continue to flow through us.

Circle all the ways His gifts are managed (administrated) well, and underline all the ways they aren't:

In order	With dignity	In chaos	In love
To manipulate	To bless	To judge	To inspire
To encourage	To condemn	To punish	To correct
To instruct	To equip	To control	

When gifts are poorly managed, believers and churches are hurt.

When spiritual gifts are managed (administrated) through a heart of service according to His will, the Holy Spirit has the freedom to move through us to touch the lives of others with God's abundant grace.

Ask yourself . . .

❖ How is the generosity of God flowing through you?

❖ How have you been giving yourself to humanity's service?

Write a prayer asking God for wisdom in managing His spiritual gifts:

_____

_____

_____

_____

_____

*G*od has given each of us the ability to do certain things well (Rom. 12:6).

God hasn't given you the ability to do everything well, because no one person can do everything He desires to be done in the church. God *has* given you the strength to face whatever circumstance you find yourself in (Phil. 4:10–14). But everyone in His church has certain strengths and certain weaknesses. What one lacks, another makes up. So we need one another as interdependent members of Christ's body—the church.

DAY 5

SPIRITUAL GIFTS:
The Ability to Do Certain Things Well

Read the following passages, and jot down *how* we need one another:

Text	How we need one another:
Romans 12:3–4	_____
1 Corinthians 12:22–27	_____
Romans 14:1–4	_____
Romans 15:1–7	_____
1 Thessalonians 5:14–22	_____
Ephesians 6:18	_____

Dependence on God and interdependence with one another should never serve as an excuse for inaction. Rather, our love and compassion for one another should prompt us to seek and use spiritual gifts to serve and build others up.

The Holy Spirit may have empowered you with one of His gifts in the past, even when you didn't realize it. Think back now to a time when the Spirit used you to minister. Then try to identify a gift He imparted to you at the time for that ministry:

To whom did you minister?_____

How did you minister? _____

What gift(s) was (were) empowered through you? _____

How did that time of ministry help the other person?_____

What does it mean to belong to one another? First, we belong to Christ (Mark 9:41). Belonging to Him puts us in the family of God (Eph. 2:19). Then, because we are members of God's family, all believers are brothers and sisters in Christ (Mark 3:35). But that doesn't mean we own or possess one another.

> *Belonging is a relationship of love that seeks another's good over my own.*

As we belong to one another in love, the Holy Spirit imparts His gifts to serve in ministry.

Ask yourself . . .

❖ To whom does the Spirit want you to minister in the power of His gifts?

❖ How does belonging to others in Christ make you accountable to living a life of purity, holiness, and integrity?

Write a prayer thanking God for the privilege of belonging to the family of God:

_____

_____

_____

_____

_____

*T*o one person the Spirit gives the ability to give wise advice . . . (1 Cor. 12:8).

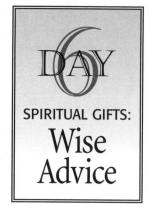

SPIRITUAL GIFTS:
Wise Advice

Wisdom is vital to living the Christian life. The gift of wisdom is the Spirit-given ability imparted to some believers to receive special insight from the Spirit so they can apply His wisdom truths to specific situations within the body of Christ.

Wisdom is seeing life from God's perspective—not our own or the world's. Scripture emphasizes the importance of godly wisdom. Read the following scriptures, and jot down what wisdom is:

1 Corinthians 1:30–2:9 _____

Proverbs 2 _____

Proverbs 8 _____

Proverbs 9 _____

Ecclesiastes 12:9–14 _____

James 1:5–8_____

2 Peter 3:15–16 _____

Picture wisdom in this way. Wisdom is the lens given by the Holy Spirit through which we view God, ourselves, our relationships, and the world around us. The Word of God is the material of which the lens is made. And our vision, or perception, is shaped and colored by the Holy Spirit's revelation. Here is the flow of wisdom:

Situation ⟶ Word of God ⟶ Vision or Perception

Shaped by the Holy Spirit ⟶ Application of Godly Wisdom

Some ways the gift of wisdom may minister through you are listed below. Check any you have knowingly encountered when the Holy Spirit empowered this gift in the body of Christ:

❑ A word of wisdom for a church problem.

❑ A word of wisdom for a family or marriage problem.

❑ A word of wisdom to clarify and guide another person through a confusing or perplexing situation.

❏ A word of wisdom to focus the attention of a person or the body on the Word of God.

❏ A word of wisdom that applies God's Word to a situation needing correction, instruction, or guidance.

❏ Other: _____

> *The gift of wisdom comes through a special gifting of the Holy Spirit, and always conforms to the whole truth of God's Word.*

Ask yourself . . .

❖ Have you ever asked God's Spirit to give you special wisdom to pray for those who need wisdom?

❖ When the Spirit guides you to share godly wisdom in a situation or with a person, are you willing to ask for humility, understanding, and kindness?

Write a prayer asking God for the Holy Spirit's special wisdom to seek His wisdom for others:

_____

_____

_____

_____

_____

*T*o another person he gives the gift of special knowledge (1 Cor. 12:8).

All special or supernatural knowledge is rooted in knowing God. Because of knowing Him, one is a candidate to be given the divine revelation of the Holy Spirit's gift of special knowledge needed by the body of Christ.

SPIRITUAL GIFTS:
Special
Knowledge

At times, an individual or church has many facts and a multitude of information, but no real spiritual insight into how to understand the whole picture. All the puzzle pieces may be there, but someone is needed who has the gift of special knowledge to put the whole picture together.

The Holy Spirit gave Peter a word of knowledge concerning Ananias and Sapphira. Now read Acts 5:1–16 and complete the following sentences:

❖ The Holy Spirit revealed to Peter the knowledge that_____

_____.

❖ The way Peter ministered this spiritual gift was to_____

_____.

❖ The church responded to the result of this word of knowledge by _____

_____.

The gift of special knowledge isn't secret or mysterious knowledge that is only revealed to a select few (Col. 2:6–23). Rather, it is a special gift that edifies, exhorts, confirms, corrects, and clarifies how the Holy Spirit is moving in the church and individual lives. When given publicly, a word of knowledge needs to be examined (1 John 4:1–6). Listed below are some criteria for examining the authenticity of special knowledge. Rank them from 1 (the most important), to 7 (the least important) as you believe them to be significant in your church:

_____ Conforms to the Word of God

_____ Confirmed by other witnesses

_____ Given under proper spiritual authority

_____ Does not judge or condemn

_____ Affirms, edifies, or speaks the truth in love

_____ Given at the prompting and release of the Holy Spirit

_____ Confesses Jesus Christ as Son of Man, Son of God, Savior, and Lord

_____ Other:_____

> *The gift of special knowledge requires the believer to be in intimate relationship with Christ through the Spirit and to be obediently listening to the Spirit's voice.*

Describe a time when someone ministered the gift of special knowledge in your life and how that word ministered to you:

_____

_____

_____

Ask yourself . . .

❖ Are you growing in a deeper knowledge and intimacy with the Lord?

❖ How does the Lord reveal special knowledge to you?

> *Write a prayer asking God's Spirit for the mind of Christ and a deeper knowledge of Him and His Word:*

_____

_____

_____

_____

_____

The Spirit gives special faith to another...
(1 Cor. 12:9).

SPIRITUAL GIFTS:

Special Faith

It is only through the grace of God's Spirit that anyone can confess Jesus Christ as Lord (1 Cor. 12:3). Ephesians 2:8 says, "God saved you by His special favor when you believed." And to believe is to have faith in God's saving favor. So true Christian faith is a decision based on the truth of God's Word. But it must also be acted upon through complete surrender and abandonment to the will of God.

There are generally two kinds of Christian faith. First, there is the faith that trusts Jesus Christ as Lord and Savior. Then there is a second, more intimate believing faith. This level of trust asks the Father to send His Holy Spirit to guide, lead, and teach us in all things so we can learn to walk by faith—not by sight (2 Cor. 5:7).

But then there is the gift of special faith that goes way beyond either of these two general kinds. The Holy Spirit's gift of faith is a special ability given by the Spirit that empowers a believer to discern and trust with extraordinary confidence the purposes of God in their church and in their lives. Those with this gift not only believe God can do the impossible, they confidently step out in a specially gifted faith to trust God in all kinds of impossible situations. The gift of faith is a spiritual impartation of radical trust in God's plan and purpose as revealed to that church or person.

Describe:

1. A time when you trusted God for the impossible: _____

_____

2. A time when your church trusted God for the impossible: _____

_____

3. A time when God moved on your behalf in response to special faith: _____

_____

Read through Hebrews 11, then briefly describe the special faith each of the following persons had:

Noah:_____

Abraham: _____

Joseph: _____

Moses: _____

Rahab: _____

The early Christians: _____

Now read Acts 27:1–44. Describe how the gift of faith empowered Paul:

_____

_____

_____

_____

> *The gift of special faith encourages the body of Christ and individuals to reach beyond their grasp; to serve beyond their abilities; to trust far beyond their sight; and to claim God's promises even when nothing in the natural suggests the possibility of fulfillment.*

Ask yourself . . .

❖ How have you been trusting God for the impossible?

❖ What keeps the gift of special faith from operating in your life?

> *Write a prayer asking God's Spirit for His gift of radical, special faith that trusts Him for the impossible:*

_____

_____

_____

_____

_____

*A*nd to someone else the power to heal the sick *(1 Cor. 12:9).*

The power to heal the sick never resides in a human being. It always rests in the power and sovereignty of God because it resides in His very nature.

Read the following passages below, and jot down what they say about God and His healing nature:

SPIRITUAL GIFTS:

Power to Heal

Exodus 15:26 _____

_____

Psalm 103:3 _____

Psalm 107:20 _____

Isaiah 53:5; 1 Peter 2:24 _____

Isaiah 61:1–3; Psalm 147:3 _____

Jeremiah 30:17 _____

Malachi 4:2 _____

Mark 2:32–34 _____

Mark 6:53–56 _____

Some who are given the gift of healing are mistakenly called "faith healers," or "healing evangelists." But the truth is that no human can heal. Only God can heal. When someone is healed through a willing vessel operating in the Spirit's power, both the one healed and the one ministering the gift should give all glory to God!

Have you ever witnessed anyone healed by the power of God? If so, describe how God's Spirit moved to heal them:

_____

_____

_____

> *The gift of the power to heal comes from the Holy Spirit and ministers through willing believers.*

The Spirit knows the deep needs of people and what in them needs healing. His spiritual gift of healing may be ministered in a number of ways. Below is a list of some of them. Circle those ways you have experienced personally or witnessed in the body of Christ:

- ❖ Laying on of hands (Mark 16:18)
- ❖ Praying for the sick (James 5:15)
- ❖ Confession of sins (James 5:16)
- ❖ Exercising faith in Christ (Luke 7:1–10; Mark 5:34)
- ❖ Believing and trusting His Word to heal (Ps. 107:20)
- ❖ Obeying *Jehovah-Rapha*—the God who heals you (Exod. 15:26)
- ❖ Commanding healing in Jesus' name (Acts 3:4–8)
- ❖ Applying the blood of Jesus Christ (1 Pet. 2:24)
- ❖ Anointing with oil (James 5:14)
- ❖ Other:_____

Does everyone touched by one who ministers in the gift of healing instantly receive physical healing? No. Anyone who ministers in the power of any of the gifts of the Spirit realizes that God can't be manipulated or controlled. In Him is healing, but He operates according to His plan—not ours. He not only wants to heal us, but He wants us to have faith and grow in understanding in our experiences. And remember: Everyone who lives and dies in Christ will one day be raised perfectly healed—body, soul, and spirit (1 Cor. 15). So every Christian will receive God's healing eventually.

Ask yourself . . .

❖ Whose healing do you need to be praying for?

❖ In what ways have you encountered healing from the Holy Spirit?

Write a prayer asking God's Spirit to use you to bring healing into the lives of others:

_____

_____

_____

_____

_____

*H*e *[the Holy Spirit] gives one person the power to perform miracles . . . (1 Cor. 12:10).*

Miracles are extraordinary events powerfully performed by God beyond the scope of natural events. They are a supernatural manifestation of the power of God.

SPIRITUAL GIFTS:

Power to Perform Miracles

The Holy Spirit did mighty miracles in the early church to demonstrate His power and salvation. Read the following scriptures, and jot down what they say about miracles:

Acts 2:22 _____

_____

Acts 2:43 _____

Acts 4:29–30 _____

Acts 5:12 _____

Acts 6:8 _____

Acts 8:6 _____

Acts 8:13 _____

Acts 14:3 _____

Acts 15:12 _____

Filled with the power of the Spirit (Luke 4:14), Jesus performed many miracles throughout His earthly ministry. And He promised that His followers would do even greater miracles than Him (John 14:12). God didn't stop working them in the early church. God wants to work miracles through you—His follower!

God demonstrated His power and presence throughout the Bible through various miracles. List five of the greatest miracles you can recall:

1. _____

2. _____

3. _____

4. _____

5. _____

God is a miracle-working God from the miracle of creation . . . to the Exodus; from Sinai and the wilderness . . . to Jericho; from the slaying of Goliath . . . to the Exile and Return; from the miracles that Jesus performed . . . to the Resurrection; and from the miracle of Pentecost . . . to the miracles of the early church—and beyond.

Describe a miracle that you have experienced through the power of the Holy Spirit.

_____

_____

> *Miracles are signs used by the Holy Spirit to point people to the miracle worker—Jesus Christ.*

As with the gift of healing power, the power to perform miracles doesn't reside in a human being. Such power comes from God's Spirit. His miracles manifest His glory for all to see. The purpose of signs (miracles) revealed in Acts 2:43 shows that, "A deep sense of awe came over them all, and the apostles performed many miraculous signs and wonders."

So miracles inspire us to reverence, praise, and give glory to God.

Ask yourself . . .

❖ What miraculous things have been empowered by His Spirit recently in your life?

❖ What miracles are you praying for now?

Write a prayer asking God's Spirit to work miraculously in the lives of those in His body:

_____

_____

_____

_____

_____

*A*nd to another the ability to prophesy . . . . Let love be your highest goal, but also desire the special abilities the Spirit gives, especially the gift of prophecy (1 Cor. 12:10, 14:1).

DAY 11

SPIRITUAL GIFTS:
Ability to Prophesy

In Hebrew, the word for prophet *(nabi)* means to be a "mouthpiece," or a "spokesman" for God. In other words, a prophet delivers the "Word of the Lord." Prophecy brings conviction, repentance, and worship to the body of Christ.

Encountering God's prophetic Word is described in 1 Corinthians 14:24–25. Read that passage, then list all that happens in the body when prophecy comes from the Lord:

1._____

2._____

3._____

4._____

5._____

This passage reveals that the main purpose of prophecy is to bring unbelievers to repentance and to a point of worshiping God. So the gift of prophecy is God's special ability to communicate His urgent truth through a yielded person in a Spirit–anointed word.

But persons claiming to minister under a prophetic anointing need to submit to the test of prophets. The criteria for examining the authenticity of a prophetic word are given in the following passages. Read each one carefully and write down what it says.

Prophetic Trust Test

1 Corinthians 14:29–33 _____

1 Corinthians 14:39–40 _____

1 John 4:1–6 _____

Deuteronomy 13:1–5 _____

Deuteronomy 18:15–22_____

Notice that false prophecy is judged harshly by the Lord. Whatever a prophet says must come to pass, or that person is a false prophet. In other words, the

Word from the Lord is always 100 percent true. So a person who claims to be a prophet and only speaks truth part of the time may be nothing more than an intellect-driven preacher, or even a psychic that utters words from other spirits. That's why Paul encourages us *not* to quench the Holy Spirit and *not* to scoff, but to test all prophecies (1 Thess. 5:19–20).

> *When ministering a prophetic word from the Lord, the Spirit of God prompts and anoints a person to speak His Word.*

So the prompting comes from the Holy Spirit, not from intellect, events, circumstances, needs, wants, or human ideas. Because a prophecy is a "God idea" not just a "good idea."

Describe a time when the Spirit inspired you with a word that encouraged, edified, and blessed another person's life:

_____

_____

_____

Ask yourself . . .

❖ What is the Spirit prophetically revealing to you?

❖ How are you proclaiming God's Word through both your words and actions?

Write a prayer asking the Holy Spirit to reveal His Word to you so you might prophetically speak and act out His Word:

_____

_____

_____

_____

_____

H *e [the Holy Spirit] gives someone else the ability to know whether it is really the Spirit of God or another spirit that is speaking (1 Cor. 12:10).*

Discernment is the special ability given by the Holy Spirit to know confidently whether or not a person claiming that a word or action is from God, is in truth from God, or satanic. Sometimes a person gifted with this ability may even see certain spirits influencing others in the spirit realm.

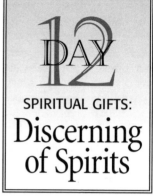

DAY 12

SPIRITUAL GIFTS:

Discerning of Spirits

Again we may turn to Acts 5:1–11 and Acts 16:16–18 to see a demonstration of this spiritual gift. Read each account, then answer these questions:

1. How did Peter know Ananias and Sapphira were lying?

_____

2. How did Paul know the origin of the spirit in the slave girl?

_____

3. What did the Holy Spirit do to Ananias and Sapphira?

_____

4. What did the Holy Spirit do to the slave girl?

_____

Read 1 John 4:1–6 and 1 Corinthians 13. Listed below are various ways the Spirit discerns through us the truth of the actions or words of another person. Check which ways the Spirit has worked in your life to discern the spirits:

❑ Listened for a confession that Jesus is the Christ, came in the flesh, died on the cross, and was raised from the dead as Lord and Savior.

❑ Observed whether the life of the person conformed to holiness or to the world.

❑ Confirmed that the actions, words, and motives of the person were guided by the Holy Spirit through faith, hope, and, most of all, love (*agape*).

❑ Discerned that the words coming from the heart of the person came from a humble, broken, and contrite heart, cleansed by the Spirit.

> *The Holy Spirit's gift of discernment empowers believers to recognize right from wrong, truth from lies, and the work of the Spirit from the work of false spirits.*

People filled with satanic spirits act certain ways. Paul describes such people in Galatians 6:16–21; 1 Timothy 6:1–6; and 2 Timothy 3:1–13. Read these Scriptures, then make a list for yourself of the things you desire the Spirit to empower you to discern:

1. _____

2. _____

3. _____

4. _____

5. _____

Ask yourself . . .

❖ How is the Holy Spirit empowering you to discern spirits?

❖ Where are you susceptible to the temptations and works of the flesh or false spirits?

> *Write a prayer asking the Holy Spirit to empower you to discern spirits through His Word and truth:*

_____

_____

_____

_____

_____

*S*till another person is given the ability to speak in unknown languages [or in tongues] (1 Cor. 12:10).

Speaking in unknown languages or tongues happened at Pentecost when the followers of Jesus were baptized with the Holy Spirit. Read Acts 2:1–21 and describe in your own words what happened when the Holy Spirit filled the believers.

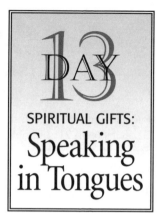

SPIRITUAL GIFTS:
Speaking in Tongues

_____

_____

_____

Unknown languages spoken by the Spirit through the believers at Pentecost were understood by people in Jerusalem from other parts of the world.

> *Speaking in tongues is the special ability given by the Holy Spirit that enables believers to speak in the language of the Spirit, and sometimes a foreign earthly language they have never learned.*

First Corinthians 13:1 says, "If I could speak in any language in heaven or on earth [in tongues of people and angels] but didn't love others, I would be only be making meaningless noise like a loud gong or clanging cymbal." So read the following passages and jot down how the Holy Spirit lovingly empowers believers to pray in the Spirit.

1 Corinthians 14:13–19 _____

1 Corinthians 12:28 _____

Acts 10:44–46 _____

Acts 19:1–7 _____

Mark 16:17_____

Romans 8:26 _____

Ephesians 6:18 _____

Jude 1:20 _____

The tongues of the Spirit may be gifted through a believer as a prophetic utterance from God in the midst of worship. When this happens, Paul instructs that the tongues should always be accompanied by interpretation (1 Cor. 14:13). Not every believer has been released to minister in every gift (1 Cor. 12:27–31). But every believer has received the gift of the Holy Spirit (Acts 2:38; 1 Cor. 3:16; Eph. 4:1–7). And within every believer is the power and potential to minister the gifts of the Holy Spirit as the sovereignty of God grants (1 Cor. 12:11).

Paul earnestly desires that all believers have the gift of speaking in tongues and that when spoken in public, there be an interpretation (1 Cor. 14:5). But he desires even more that all prophesy so everyone can understand God's Word. We will explore the gift of interpretation of tongues in the next devotional study.

❖ Have you ever asked the Spirit to give you the gift of tongues?_____

_____

❖ If so, why did you ask? (Note 1 Cor. 14:1.)_____

_____

❖ How did God respond to your request?_____

_____

Ask yourself . . .

❖ How is the Holy Spirit speaking and praying through me?

❖ In what ways have I been ministered to through the gift of tongues?

Write a prayer asking the Holy Spirit to empower you to speak and pray as He desires:

_____

_____

_____

_____

_____

*S*till another person is given the ability to speak in unknown languages [or in tongues], and another is given the ability to interpret what is being said (1 Cor. 12:10).

The gift of interpreting tongues is given by the Holy Spirit to believers to make known the meaning of His gifted utterance when spoken to the body.

Read the following passages and write down what they say about the gift of interpreting tongues:

SPIRITUAL GIFTS:

Interpreting Tongues

1 Corinthians 12:30 _____

1 Corinthians 14:13 _____

1 Corinthians 14:26–28 _____

When God speaks to the body through tongues, an interpretation of those tongues must be given. The Holy Spirit will reveal to a believer what the message meant and will have that person interpret the tongue in a language that all can understand. Without the gift of interpretation, the gift of tongues given in public worship can be misunderstood and very confusing.

Read 1 Corinthians 14:5–25 and make a list of the needs that Paul gives for the gift of interpretation:

1. _____

2. _____

3. _____

4. _____

5. _____

Have you ever encountered tongues and interpretation in a worship service? Have you personally ever received a prophecy in tongues? Has the Holy Spirit ever gifted you with the interpretation of tongues?

If any of the preceding questions were answered yes by you, what were some of the feelings you experienced when it (they) occurred: (Circle all that apply.)

Fear	Expectancy	Skepticism	Anticipation
Joy	Confusion	Gratitude	Frustration

Other: _____

Now in one sentence, write about any special experience or encounter you may have had with tongues and interpretation that wonderfully encouraged you:

_____

_____

When tongues and the interpretation of tongues occur in a public service, they are to be presented properly and in order (1 Cor. 14:40). Describe how your congregation and pastor handle tongues and interpretation in worship:

_____

_____

> *Tongues and interpretation of tongues are given by the Spirit to encourage, edify, instruct, and guide the body of Christ with an immediate word from the Lord that always conforms to and confirms the Word of God.*

Ask yourself . . .

❖ When have you been encouraged by an interpretation of tongues in worship?

❖ How would you respond if the Holy Spirit gave you an interpretation of tongues?

Write a prayer asking the Holy Spirit to interpret tongues through you whenever He so desires:

_____

_____

_____

_____

*H*e is the one who gave these gifts to the church: the apostles ... (Eph. 4:11).

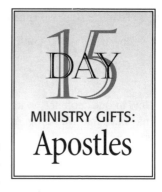

An apostle is *one who is sent.* Apostles are missionaries and church planters who establish God's work in cultures around the world.

MINISTRY GIFTS:
Apostles

An apostle may be sent across town or across the ocean to establish a church where there is none. Apostles operate in many spiritual giftings so they can raise up new Christians and leaders in the power of the Spirit.

An apostle or missionary may go into a new area to plant numerous churches. Years after they are established the apostle may not actually pastor his planted works, but is pastor to those pastors. That's why some church leaders are referred to as having "apostolic authority." The term simply refers to the calling and experience these anointed ministers exercised when pioneering new works, to their initiating rights as overseers of the new leaders, and to their original vision in the planting of the church.

The following passages describe some of the ministry assignments of an apostle. Read them, then jot down what the Holy Spirit does through apostles.

Acts 8:4–5 _____

Acts 13:2–3 _____

Acts 22:21_____

Romans 10:15 _____

1 Corinthians 9:19–23 _____

Now name some apostles or missionaries you have known and briefly describe their ministries.

Apostles	Their Ministries
_____	_____
_____	_____
_____	_____
_____	_____

For those not called and sent by the Holy Spirit as apostles, we still have a commission to take the gospel wherever we go (Matt. 28:18–20). We can also do the following things to support one who is sent as an apostle. After reflecting a bit on this section, check which of the following you can and will do.

❑ Financial support of mission work.

❑ Use my gifts to work in missions.

❑ Pray for missionaries.

❑ Learn all I can about the need for and how to plant new mission works.

❑ Ask the Lord to provide the means for you to go on mission trips.

❑ Other:

Ask yourself . . .

❖ What apostles am I praying for and supporting?

❖ How is God using me as a missionary?

Write a prayer asking the Holy Spirit to teach you how to pray for apostles:

_____

_____

_____

_____

_____

H *e is the one who gave these gifts to the church: the apostles, the prophets, and the evangelists ... (Eph. 4:11).*

Evangelists are gifted by the Holy Spirit to share the gospel of Christ in such a way that men and women repent, are born again, and become disciples of Christ. So an evangelist is one with a special anointing to proclaim the good news of Jesus Christ.

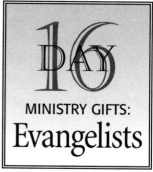

DAY 16

MINISTRY GIFTS:

Evangelists

The gift of evangelism may be imparted to any in a time of leading an unbeliever to Christ. But those who are called to the office of evangelism spend their lives proclaiming the gospel everywhere God leads them to go. There is a special gifting in this ministry gift to draw unbelievers to the Savior.

List three or four evangelists you have heard and been ministered to through their evangelistic gift.

_____

_____

_____

_____

Has God ever used you to evangelize another person? If so, describe the empowering experience given through the Holy Spirit that led that person to Christ:

_____

_____

There are many examples of evangelists and evangelism in the New Testament. Read the following scriptures, and jot down what you learn about the evangelistic gift:

Acts 8:5–6 _____

Acts 8:26–40 _____

Acts 14:21_____

Acts 21:8 _____

2 Timothy 4:5 _____

While you may not exercise the gift of evangelism through full-time ministry, you will need the power to operate in this gift whenever you meet unsaved people. But many resist God's soulwinning power for one reason or another. What keeps this gift from being stirred up in you through the Holy Spirit? Rank from 1 (the greatest obstacle), to 5 (the least obstacle) to evangelism in you:

_____ Fear of rejection

_____ Not knowing what to say

_____ Worried about looking foolish

_____ Unable to say the right words

_____ Untrained or ill-equipped to share the gospel

> *The Holy Spirit both raises up evangelists for the masses and stirs up the gift of evangelism within individuals to reach the lost for Jesus Christ.*

Ask yourself . . .

❖ Which evangelists do you pray for and support?

❖ How is the Lord using the gift of evangelism in you to reach the lost?

Write a prayer asking the Holy Spirit to give you a heart and compassion for the lost:

_____

_____

_____

_____

_____

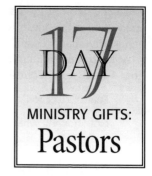

*H*e is the one who gave these gifts to the church: the apostles, the prophets, the evangelists, and the pastors and teachers (Eph. 4:11).

A pastor is a shepherd and nurturer of God's flock. The anointing and calling for this gift is rooted in the Chief Shepherd—Jesus Christ (Heb. 13:20–21). A pastor, or shepherd, assumes responsibility for the spiritual welfare of the sheep in the church entrusted by the Spirit into his care.

Read 2 Timothy 2:14–26 and Psalm 23. Then write on the sheep below some of the ways a shepherd cares for sheep.

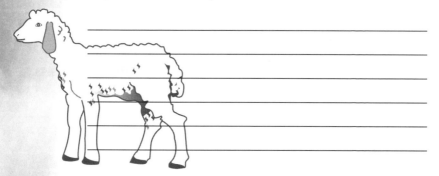

The gift of pastoring people involves nurturing and caring for them as well as correcting and rebuking. Pastors become intimately involved in the lives of their sheep. They often set aside their own needs to care for the needs of the flock.

Think of all the pastors gifted by the Holy Spirit that you have known. Now rank the responsibilities you deem most important (1), to least important (7) for pastors:

_____A heart for God

_____Filled and empowered by the Holy Spirit

_____Devoted to the study and proclamation of the Word

_____One who prays and intercedes for the flock

_____One who visits the sick, shut-in, imprisoned, poor, and lonely

_____Preaching and teaching the Word

_____Training and equipping the saints

_____One who has a godly marriage and family

_____Other:_____

The person called and anointed by the Spirit of God to pastor may be involved in the responsibilities listed above full time. But all believers are called to minister and care for one another (1 Cor. 12:25–26).

Complete the following sentences:

❖ One way I minister to other believers is _____

_____.

❖ The Holy Spirit has gifted me to nurture others by _____

_____.

❖ One thing that keeps me from nurturing other believers is _____

_____.

> *Pastors are God's chosen healers of the wounded and living reminders in the body of Christ of the great Shepherd—Jesus Christ.*

Ask yourself . . .

❖ How are you leading and nurturing other believers?

❖ How are you supporting your pastor(s)?

Write a prayer interceding for pastors:

_____

_____

_____

_____

_____

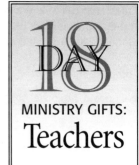

*H*e is the one who gave these gifts to the church: the apostles, the prophets, the evangelists, and the pastors and teachers (Eph. 4:11).

Teachers are gifted by the Holy Spirit to communicate biblical truths to believers in such a powerful way that they dynamically learn how to live the Christian life as disciples of Christ.

Some people may have learned teaching skills, but they aren't Holy Spirit-gifted teachers of the Word. Just because a person is a skilled teacher in the natural doesn't mean that he or she is gifted in teaching spiritual things.

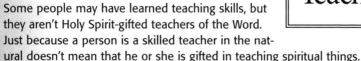

One who is gifted by the Spirit in teaching is able to dynamically communicate biblical truths in both understandable and applicable ways to believers.

Scripture places a high value on the gift of teaching. The One who inspires teaching is the Holy Spirit. Examine what the Bible says about teaching and jot down what you learn:

Deuteronomy 6:4–7 _____

Matthew 28:19–20 _____

Romans 12:7 _____

1 Corinthians 14:26 _____

2 Corinthians 10:5 _____

Colossians 1:28 _____

Colossians 3:16 _____

1 Timothy 3:2, 4:11–12 _____

2 Timothy 2:23–25 _____

2 Timothy 3:16 _____

Titus 2:2–3 _____

James 3:1 _____

1 John 2:27 _____

Jesus only did and spoke what the Father did and spoke. And the Spirit only does and speaks what the Son asks Him to do and speak. So both Jesus and the Spirit are perfect examples for the teachers they call. Jesus is called *Rabbi*, and He in turn reveals through the Spirit the truth He teaches us. The Spirit imparts the gift of teaching to the one who follows the Spirit, who follows Jesus, who in turn follows the Father.

Jot down what the following verses say concerning the ways we are to teach by example:

Be an example . . .

John 13:5–14 _____

Acts 20:35 _____

1 Corinthians 4:16, 11:1 _____

Ephesians 5:1–2 _____

Philippians 3:17 _____

1 Thessalonians 1: 7 _____

2 Thessalonians 3:7–9 _____

1 Timothy 4:12 _____

> *Through the gift of teaching the Holy Spirit empowers teachers to equip the saints by example, holy, and pure attitudes, spiritual disciplines, study of the Word, prayer, servanthood, and the practice of the presence of God.*

Ask yourself . . .

❖ How is the Holy Spirit making your life an example to other believers?

❖ Who is teaching you in the ways of the Lord?

Write a prayer interceding for teachers:

_____

_____

_____

*I*f your gift is that of serving others, serve them well (Rom. 12:7).

All believers are called to be servants (Phil. 2). But there is a special ability given by the Spirit to some believers called the gift of helps. This gift empowers believers to invest their time and abilities in the life and ministry of the body so other believers can become more effective in using their gifts.

Recall a time when another Christian served and helped you enabling you to use your gift(s) more effectively. Describe that time:

_____

_____

The gift of serving others, or helps, is described in the following passages. Read each passage and jot down what you learn about this spiritual gift:

1 Corinthians 12:28 _____

Mark 15:40–41 _____

Luke 8:2–3 _____

Acts 6:1–7_____

Acts 9:36 _____

Romans 16:1–2 _____

Serving requires certain attitudes that allow the Holy Spirit to use us in ministry. To minister is to serve. So there is no ministry without a servant's heart. Below is a heart. Write on it all the attitudes you believe a servant needs in order to minister help to others:

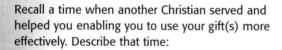

_____

_____

_____

_____

_____

Look at your list. Be certain it includes such qualities as love, humility, generosity, joy, and obedience. Now circle the qualities that most need to grow in your own life as a servant.

> *The gift of serving (helps) simply takes the qualities of service beyond the normal to the radical. Those with this gifting go to the extreme—far beyond the expected—in ministering to others.*

Helps ministers are willing to sacrifice all self-interest and resources to help others with their ministries. At the same time, they don't expect recognition, glory, or rewards.

List some of those you know with the gifts of helps who are serving others. Write next to their name how they demonstrate their gift.

Name   **How they use their gift**

_____   _____

_____   _____

_____   _____

Ask yourself . . .

❖ How are others helping you to minister in your gifts?

❖ In what ways are you serving other believers?

Write a prayer thanking God for those with the gift of helps to serve others:

_____

_____

_____

_____

_____

*I*f your gift is to encourage others, do it! (Rom 12:8).

DAY 20

BODY GIFTS:

Encouragement

Everyone needs encouragement. Acceptance and affirmation are important in the body of Christ. And all of us need to regularly affirm others. But there is a special ability given by the Holy Spirit for the encouragement, or exhorting, of believers who need comfort, consolation, and counsel.

Encouragement recognizes strengths without focusing on weaknesses or faults. One with the gift of encouragement has the ability to build up others instead of tearing them down.

The encouragement of the Holy Spirit strengthens the body to help Christians face difficult trials and problems in life. Jot down what these passages say about the gift of encouragement (exhortation):

Acts 14:21–22 _____

Hebrews 10:25 _____

1 Timothy 4:13 _____

When someone with the gift of encouragement ministers to you, how do you feel? Circle all the feelings you have:

Comforted   Confident

Affirmed   Loved

Nurtured   Other: _____

> *Since the Holy Spirit is the Comforter, Encourager, and Counselor (paraclete), the gift of encouragement is actually releasing the Holy Spirit within a believer to minister to another's deepest needs.*

The best example in Scripture of someone with this gift is Barnabas. Read these passages about Barnabas, then write a paragraph profile that describes an encourager: (Acts 4:36–37, 11:22–30; Acts 13:15).

An encourager _____

_____

_____

_____

The Holy Spirit may prompt you to help someone without any indication from them that they need help. When this happens, don't rush in and start helping. Rather, pray for the Holy Spirit to prepare their hearts to receive God's help. Then ask permission to help. Be an encourager without any thought of gratitude or appreciation from those to whom you minister. And never forget to praise God for the opportunity to encourage.

Ask yourself . . .

❖ Who is the Spirit prompting you to encourage? What is He asking you to do?

❖ Are you yielded to the Spirit so He may stir up within you the gift of encouragement?

Write a prayer asking God's Spirit to use you in encouraging others:

_____

_____

_____

_____

_____

C heerfully share your home with those who need a meal or a place to stay. God has given gifts to each of you from his great variety of spiritual gifts. Manage them well so that God's generosity can flow through you (1 Pet. 4:9–10).

BODY GIFTS:

Hospitality

Some Christians have the special ability to prepare their homes and meals to show hospitality to guests. They are gifted by the Holy Spirit to serve the physical needs of people and love to provide an open and inviting home to minister to others.

Do you have this gift? Put an *x* on the line where you are:

Prepare food for others

_____

Love to   It's a chore

Clean the house for company

_____

Love to   It's a chore

Do laundry for guests

_____

Love to   It's a chore

Decorate home or church for guests _____

Love to   It's a chore

The gift of hospitality is mentioned throughout the New Testament. Here are the passages that discuss it. Read each one then check whether or not it describes you.

Hospitality	Describes Me	Not Me
Romans 12:13	❑	❑
Romans 16:23	❑	❑
1 Timothy 3:2	❑	❑
Titus 1:8	❑	❑
Hebrews 13:2, 16	❑	❑

The gift of hospitality empowers a believer to perceive, anticipate, and cheerfully minister to the physical needs of strangers or other believers. Those so gifted by the Holy Spirit cheerfully minister to people's needs of food and lodging without feeling duty-bound or resenting the sacrifice required.

Ask yourself . . .

❖ In what ways has the Holy Spirit inspired you to be hospitable?

❖ What people do you know who have this gift?

Write a prayer asking God's Spirit to help you understand and meet the needs of food and lodging others may have:

_____

_____

_____

_____

_____

*I*f you have money, share it generously *(Rom. 12:8).*

The Holy Spirit gifts some members of Christ's body to give far beyond a tithe. Those inspired with this gift contribute their material resources generously and cheerfully far beyond the regular contributions of most believers.

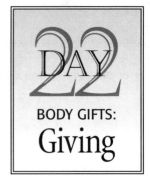

DAY 22

BODY GIFTS:
Giving

We might say that there are three types of givers:

❖ *Dutiful*—Those who give out of obligation to satisfy their consciences and obey God's commands to give.
❖ *Sacrificial*—Those who give until it hurts. They willingly do without things and personal comforts in order to give to God's work.
❖ *Cheerful*—Those who have grown beyond dutiful and sacrificial giving to the point of regarding giving as a joy and privilege.

> *Those gifted to give, not only give cheerfully, they also generously seek out new opportunities to give.*

Gifted givers seek out opportunities to give instead of waiting for requests to come to them. They search for worthwhile ministries in which to invest their resources for a harvest in the kingdom of God.

When you give beyond your regular giving or immediate resources, how do you feel? Circle any one of the following:

Resentful	Joyful	Lacking	Excited
Pleased	Obedient	Manipulated	Generous

Other: _____

Complete the following sentences:

I give _____ percent of my income to the work of the Lord.

I give _____ percent of my waking time to the work of the Lord.

The percent of my time I spend at work is _____.

The percent of my skills and talents I use for God is _____.

God is a giver. He gave His only Son to die for us (John 3:16). And He gave His

Holy Spirit to empower us with new life and to make us His witnesses in the world (Acts 1). So what keeps us from giving with the same generosity as God?

_____ Fear of losing what we have.

_____ We don't really appreciate Him.

_____ We give out of duty not love.

_____ Other:_____

Ask yourself . . .

❖ In what ways have you encountered the gift of giving within or around you?

❖ Who around you has this gift?

Write a prayer asking God's Spirit to help you become a giver:

_____

_____

_____

_____

_____

*I*f God has given you leadership ability, take the responsibility seriously (Rom. 12:8).

Leadership is the Spirit-given ability to grasp God's vision for His people. But leadership does more than just "grasp." This ability can communicate that vision to Christ's body in a way that produces unity and accomplishes the vision for the glory of God.

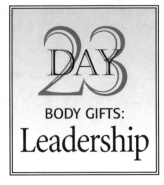

DAY 23

BODY GIFTS:
Leadership

The Spirit empowers a godly leader to become an example for others to follow. What attributes have you observed in the Spirit-filled leaders you have known: (Check all that apply.)

❏ Knowledge of God's Word   ❏ Wisdom

❏ Holiness and purity   ❏ Faith

❏ One who prays and intercedes ❏ Integrity

❏ Humble dependence upon God   ❏ Patience

❏ Ability to communicate clearly ❏ Inspires others

❏ Promotes unity and love   ❏ Listens

❏ Has the flesh under self-control ❏ Affirms others

❏ Hears from God   ❏ Walks his talk

❏ Transparent and vulnerable   ❏ Courageous

❏ Serves others selflessly   ❏ Other:_____

A Spirit-led leader puts aside personal gain and glory for the vision given him or her by the Holy Spirit.

Below is a list of leaders from the Bible. Which of them inspire you most? (Check your six most inspiring leaders in the Scriptures.)

❏ Paul   ❏ Peter   ❏ Lydia

❏ Deborah   ❏ Moses   ❏ Joshua

❏ Joseph   ❏ David   ❏ Hezekiah

❏ Ruth   ❏ Hannah   ❏ Abraham

❏ Josiah   ❏ Daniel   ❏ Mary

❏ Stephen   ❏ Priscilla   ❏ Elijah

❏ Others: _____

Now read the following scriptures, then jot down the qualities they ascribe to godly leaders:

Luke 9:62 _____

Acts 7:10 _____

Acts 15:7–11 _____

Hebrews 13:17 _____

1 Timothy 5:17 _____

The source of strength, truth, holiness, and servanthood in leadership is the Holy Spirit. When He overflows and anoints a life, that person will lead not by might, nor by power, but by the Spirit (Zech. 4:6).

Ask yourself . . .

❖ Who has the Spirit put in my life as a gifted leader?

❖ How is the Holy Spirit using me as a leader?

Write a prayer interceding for spiritual leaders:

_____

_____

_____

_____

_____

A *nd if you have a gift for showing kindness to others, do it gladly (Rom. 12:8).*

Kindness, or mercy, is the special ability given by the Holy Spirit to some believers who show Jesus' genuine empathy and compassion toward others who may be suffering physically, emotionally, mentally, or spiritually.

All believers have compassion and express lovingkindness toward those in need. But believers gifted with the Spirit's kindness deeply feel the

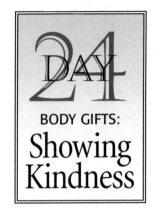

BODY GIFTS:

Showing Kindness

pain and hurt of others to minister His comfort to the hurting. They are spiritually empowered to find needs to meet and hurts to heal.

Read over the following passages then jot down what they reveal about the gift of kindness:

Matthew 20:29–34 _____

Mark 9:41 _____

Luke 10:30–35_____

Acts 11:28–30 _____

Acts 16:33–34 _____

Which kinds of persons with needs most prompt the gift of mercy and kindness within you? (Check all that apply.)

Those physically handicapped	Mentally ill	Poor
Elderly	Shut-in	Prisoners
Sick	Homeless	Hungry
Abused	Orphaned	The unborn

Other: _____

Have you ever received ministry from someone with the gift of kindness? If so, describe the situation:

When I was in need, _____

_____.

After ministry, I experienced _____

_____.

What most blocks the gift of kindness in your life? Circle those things that keep the Spirit's special kindness from flowing through your life:

Fear of getting involved	Not knowing what to do
Lack of sensitivity	Too busy
Too bound by my own problems	Other: _____

Ask yourself . . .

❖ Who has ministered God's special kindness to you?

❖ Who needs the Spirit's kindness (mercy) to flow through you to them?

Write a prayer asking the Spirit to fill you with the kindness and compassion of Jesus Christ:

_____

_____

_____

_____

_____

E *paphras, from your city, a servant of Christ Jesus, sends you his greetings. He always prays earnestly for you, asking God to make you strong and perfect, fully confident of the whole will of God (Col. 4:12).*

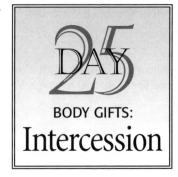

BODY GIFTS:

Intercession

Some believers in the body are gifted and empowered by the Holy Spirit to pray always and unceasingly for extended periods of time. These gifted intercessors see God respond in mighty ways to their prayers, even beyond the level regularly experienced by other believers.

One key for recognizing this gifting is the persistency and constancy of prayer maintained by a believer. The Holy Spirit gifted Epaphras and Paul to pray always and unceasingly for others. Read the following passages that refer to the ongoing intercession of God's prayer warriors and jot down how they prayed:

Text	They interceded . . . .
Acts 12:12	_____
Colossians 1:9–12	_____
Ephesians 6:18	_____
1 Timothy 2:1–2	_____
James 5:14–16	_____

When asked to pray for someone, some believers may pray once or twice, then go on to something else. Some may even forget to pray. But the gifted intercessor will often pray all day.

> *Those gifted as intercessors grab hold of the altar of prayer and refuse to stop interceding until God answers.*

Intercessors persist in prayer and at times even fast when others have given up.

The Holy Spirit counsels and empowers us in intercession. Read Romans 8:26–27, then paraphrase it in your own words:

_____

_____

Below is a list of some of the qualities in those who intercede. Check those you have now, and circle those you desire the Spirit to cultivate in you:

❏ Patience   ❏ Perseverance

❏ Being still before God   ❏ Always praying

❏ Seeking God's face   ❏ Thirsting for God's Presence

❏ Setting aside personal prayer needs for the needs of others

❏ Continuing in prayer in spite of hunger, fatigue, or other distractions

❏ Silencing all other voices except God's voice

Ask yourself . . .

❖ To whom would you go to ask for their intercession?

❖ Are you willing to allow the Spirit to grow you into becoming an intercessor?

Write a prayer of intercession asking the Holy Spirit to tell you whom to pray for and what their needs are:

_____

_____

_____

_____

_____

O *ur hearts ache, but we always have joy. We are*
poor, but we give spiritual riches to others. We
own nothing, and yet we have everything
(2 Cor. 6:10).

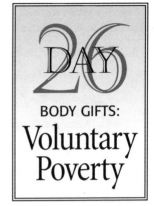

BODY GIFTS:
Voluntary Poverty

Throughout Christian history, there have been
believers who have been gifted by the Holy Spirit
to embrace poverty as a vessel for ministry. Francis
of Assisi, Albert Sweitzer, and Mother Teresa are
three of the best-known Christian leaders to have
ever been used like this. They didn't deny that God
would materially bless people. They simply heard
God's Spirit say to them, "Go and sell all you have
and give the money to the poor, and you will have treasure in heaven. Then
come, follow me" (Mark 10:21).

Paul surrendered wealth, position, status, and a leadership position among his
own people to follow Christ.

> *Voluntary poverty is the spiritual gift given by the Spirit to*
> *some believers that empowers them to renounce material*
> *comfort and luxury while embracing a lifestyle of poverty*
> *so they can minister more effectively to others.*

If the Holy Spirit asked you to embrace this gift because of the area He was
sending you to, or the uniqueness of your call, what would be the hardest
thing for you to give away? Check the three hardest things to give up:

_____ House

_____ Good and abundant food

_____ Vehicles

_____ Television, computer, or electronic equipment

_____ Sports or leisure vehicles

_____ Travel

_____ Entertainment

_____ A high paying job

_____ Other:_____

Look up the following scriptures about voluntary poverty, and write down what they say to you:

Acts 2:44–45 _____

Acts 4:34–37 _____

1 Corinthians 13:1–3 _____

2 Corinthians 6:10, 8:9 _____

Ask yourself . . .

❖ How would you respond if the Spirit asked you to give up your material possessions to be more effectively used by Him?

❖ How will you minister to those who have the gift of voluntary poverty?

Write a prayer thanking God for all those in history whose gift of voluntary poverty has blessed you, then offer your availability if this is God's will for you:

_____

_____

_____

_____

_____

*T*hose who can get others to work together ... *(1 Cor. 12:28).*

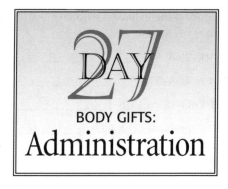

BODY GIFTS:
Administration

The gift of administration is given by the Holy Spirit to some believers to understand and implement specific tasks or goals in the body of Christ. These Holy Spirit-gifted administrators can minister in such a way that people work together efficiently, harmoniously, and joyfully.

Those gifted with administration oil the machinery of ministry with an anointing of love, wisdom, practicality, and knowledge. They are often behind the scenes organizing and inspiring others to work together in accomplishing important visible tasks within the body of Christ.

Check the following areas in which you have seen the gift of administration at work:

_____ Constructing buildings and facilities

_____ Managing finances and budgets

_____ Overseeing staff

_____ Setting goals and planning tasks

_____ Supporting leadership by taking care of details

_____ Mobilizing small groups and committees to do ministry

_____ Setting up effective communication among all members of the body

_____ Other:_____

Read the following passages, then summarize in one sentence what they reveal about the gift of administration (Luke 14:28–30; Acts 6:1–7; Titus 1:5).

_____

_____

_____

_____

The Holy Spirit's gift of administration inspires people to work together in unity in the body of Christ. The one gifted in this area will not only organize for the body's good, but will possess a special anointing to bond believers together in love.

Read John 17. This is Jesus' prayer for the church. List all the points Jesus makes about unity and oneness in the church:

_____

_____

_____

_____

Without those gifted to help believers work together there is division and strife in the church.

Ask yourself . . .

❖ How can you support those with the gift of administration?

❖ How has the Spirit gifted you to help believers work together?

Write a prayer asking God's Spirit to use you in maintaining unity in the church:

_____

_____

_____

_____

_____

I *wish everyone could get along without marrying,*
just as I do. But we are not all the same. God gives
some the gift of marriage, and to others he gives
the gift of singleness (1 Cor. 7:7).

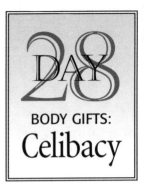

BODY GIFTS:
Celibacy

Not all single people have been called as celibates
to minister in the power of the Spirit. People remain
or become single for a variety of reasons. But
celibacy is a gift from God.

The Holy Spirit empowers certain believers to
remain single and enjoy being single without suffering undue sexual temptations.

> *Celibate believers are empowered by the Spirit to*
> *devote significant time and effort to ministry without*
> *the responsibilities of a spouse and family.*

Read Matthew 19:10–12. In one sentence paraphrase what this text says to
you about being single.

_____

_____

Think of the single people you have known who are effective ministers in the
body of Christ. Now write down their names and the ministries they have
served the Lord with:

Single persons	**Their ministry**
_____	_____
_____	_____
_____	_____

There is one advantage attached to being single. Singleness can be a liberating
factor in accomplishing many things in ministry that marriage could hinder.
Think of three blessings that being single could be to a ministry and list them.

1._____

2._____

3._____

Now consider some of the difficulties single persons face in ministry within the church. Check those things you think would be most difficult:

_____ Loneliness

_____ Sexual temptation

_____ Lack of understanding about marriage

_____ Isolation

_____ Judgmental attitudes from married believers

_____ Other:_____

If you are single, are you willing to consider the Holy Spirit's gift of celibacy to empower your ministry?

If you are married, are you willing to encourage singles you know to consider the possibility that their celibacy may be a gift from God?

Ask yourself . . .

❖ How are you encouraging and affirming the ministry giftings in singles you know?

❖ How has this study changed or altered your view of single persons in ministry?

Write a prayer thanking God for those who have the gift of celibacy:

_____

_____

_____

_____

_____

*T*hey will cast out demons in my name
(Mark 16:17).

While many believers may not often encounter the need to cast out demons today, it is a powerful and necessary gift of the Spirit that destroys the devil's work.

BODY GIFTS:
Exorcism

Read the following passages and describe how this gifts works:

Matthew 12:22–32 _____

Luke 10:17–20_____

Acts 8:5–8_____

Acts 16:16–18 _____

Scripture warns us to stand firm against "those mighty powers of darkness who rule this world, and against wicked spirits in the heavenly realms," and that we are to "use every piece of God's armor to resist the enemy in the time of evil" (Eph. 6:12–13).

> *The person gifted in exorcism knows*
> *how to put on the armor of God.*

Read Ephesians 6:10–18, and write a brief description of each part of armor, describing how it is used to resist, oppose, and cast out demons.

_____

_____

_____

_____

_____

_____

_____

The following Scriptures will reveal the fact that there truly are evil spirits that oppress and possess people. So even if you aren't gifted by the Spirit to cast out demons and evil spirits, you should recognize the enemy when he attacks

(2 Cor. 2:11). Read the text, then identify the type of demon, its activities when mentioned, and how it was dealt with.

Matthew 8:16, 10:1, 12:43–45 _____

Mark 1:23–27, 3:11, 29–30 _____

Mark 5:2–13, 6:7 _____

Mark 7:25, 9:17–29 _____

Luke 8:2, 10:20 _____

Luke 11:24–26 _____

Luke 13:11–13 _____

Acts 5:16, 8:6–7, 19:13–15 _____

Ask yourself . . .

❖ When faced with an evil spirit or demon, are you willing to let the Holy Spirit empower you to cast it out?

Write a prayer asking the Holy Spirit to give you discernment of evil spirits and the boldness to cast them out in Jesus' name:

_____

_____

_____

_____

_____

*H*owever, he has given each one of us a special gift according to the generosity of Christ (Eph. 4:7).

BODY GIFTS:

Special Gifts

To each believer is given a special gift according to the grace of Christ. It is our hope that you now understand some of your spiritual giftings in the body of Christ.

If all of your gifts are dormant, ask Christ to anoint and baptize you with the Holy Spirit. He will empower you with His giftings to minister effectively in the body of Christ.

Now as you conclude your study, complete these sentences:

❖ One new thing I learned in this study is _____

_____.

❖ One gift operating with power in my life is _____

_____.

❖ One exciting way the Holy Spirit is beginning to work in and through me is

_____

_____

_____.

❖ The most powerful encounter I had with the Holy Spirit during this study was

_____

_____

_____.

> *All believers have been empowered by the indwelling Holy Spirit to minister in His special gifts. That includes you!*

Ask yourself . . .

❖ Am I willing to yield to the baptism and power of the Holy Spirit indwelling me to release whatever special gift(s) He desires to release through me in ministry?

Write a prayer praising God for the Holy Spirit and His special gifts:

_____

_____

_____

_____

_____

You can continue your encounters with the Holy Spirit by using the other devotional study guides listed at the end of this booklet, and by using the companion *Holy Spirit Encounter Bible.*

Leader's Guide

For Group Sessions

This devotional study is an excellent resource for group study including such settings as:

- ❖ Sunday school classes and other church classes
- ❖ Prayer groups
- ❖ Bible study groups
- ❖ Ministries involving small groups, home groups, and accountability groups
- ❖ Study groups for youth and adults

Before the First Session

- ❖ Contact everyone interested in participating in your group to inform them about the meeting time, date, and place.
- ❖ Make certain that everyone has a copy of this devotional study guide.
- ❖ Plan out all your teaching lessons before starting the first session. Also ask group members to begin their daily encounters in this guide. While each session will not strictly adhere to a seven-day schedule, group members who faithfully study a devotional every day will be prepared to share in the group sessions.
- ❖ Pray for the Holy Spirit to guide, teach, and help each participant.
- ❖ Be certain the place where you meet has a chalkboard, white board, or flipchart with appropriate writing materials.

Planning the Group Sessions

1. You will have four sessions together as a group. So plan to cover at least seven days in each session. If your sessions are weekly, ask the participants to complete the final two days before the last session.

2. In your first session, have group members find a partner with whom they will share and pray each time you meet. Keep the same pairs throughout the group sessions. See if you can randomly put pairs together—men with men, and women with women.

3. Have group and class members complete their devotional studies prior to their group sessions to enhance group sharing, study, and prayer. Begin each session with prayer.

4. Either the group leader or selected members should read the key Scriptures from each of the seven daily devotionals you will be studying in the session.

5. As the leader, you should decide which exercises and questions are to be covered prior to each session.

6. Also decide which exercises and sessions will be most appropriate to share with the group as a whole, or in pairs.

7. Decide which prayer(s) from the seven devotionals you will want the pairs to pray with one another.

8. Close each session by giving every group member the opportunity to share with the group how he or she encountered the Holy Spirit during the previous week. Then lead the group in prayer or have group members pray aloud in a prayer circle as you close the session.

9. You will have nine days of devotionals to study in the last session. So, use the last day as an in-depth sharing time in pairs. Invite all the group members to share the most important thing they learned about the Holy Spirit's gifts during this study and how their relationship with the Spirit was deepened because of it. Close with prayers of praise and thanksgiving.

10. Remember to allow each person the freedom "not to share" with their prayer partner or in public if they are uncomfortable with it.

11. Always start and end each group session on time and seek to keep them no longer than ninety minutes.

12. Finally, be careful. This is not a therapy group. Group members who seek to dominate group discussions with their own problems or questions should be ministered to by the group leader or pastor one-on-one outside of the group session.

Titles in the Holy Spirit
Encounter Guide Series

Additional Notes

Additional Notes

Additional Notes

Additional Notes

Additional Notes

Additional Notes

Additional Notes

Additional Notes

Additional Notes

Additional Notes